Nation – Country

(October 2016)

*

essay

*

Traumear

Paperback ISBN 978-0-244-63804-7

*

www.traumear.com

*

This essay is an attempt to give those something to aim for who painfully experience the increasing disconnect between, on one side, the never-ending struggle for national self-sufficiency and for international supremacy and on the other side the eternal wish by self-governing, communal human beings to live in countries that get along decently, imaginatively and even magnanimously with other countries.

*

Nation – Country

International politics is first and foremost a set of survival strategies. From that point of view we may tend to think of *the world*, nowadays perhaps more than ever, as a competitive struggle for survival. If the wish for supremacy plays into it, then this may stem partly from arrogance, but above all else it would seem to guarantee a period, at least, of rest from that struggle. There seems to be no way out of this incessant back and forth between momentary advantage and unavoidable set-back until it dawns on us that survival is not life. This never seems to dawn on more than a few of us at a time. It is up to these few then to persuade a few more of what they understand.

When a segment of the earth's population declares itself to be a nation, or to continue to be a nation, something is at work which can be called world-spirit. The essence of this world-spirit is communal human being. To the degree that we cooperate with it we become communal human beings, which is to say we welcome the threat to our egos, to our selfishness and self-centredness and embrace those in our vicinity respectfully, honourably and lovingly.

So world-spirit challenges our selfishness. This is not the intention of world-spirit, however it is bound to happen to the extent that we do not welcome this spirit but instead cling to our self. Equally we may sensibly understand all challenges to our self-interest as guarantee that world-spirit is available to us but we have, to the extent of our pain and discomfort, not yet welcomed it.

1

We lose nothing and gain everything by welcoming world-spirit. We gain first and foremost our stature as real human beings and in addition we live, which implies that we love and are loved.

We tend to react when our self is challenged. We may of course notice this and decide to respond, and to co-respond, right away. The sooner the better. If instead we continue to re-act, we automatically produce mythic enemies for ourselves, against whom we require protection. For one example, we seek protection in numbers. A crowd of the like-minded most readily serves. Tribes, classes, dynasties, families and houses – all these do principally offer a spurious security against mythic enemies. They are social, not communal entities. They are based on fear and hatred of an enemy and they are supposed to offer protection against that enemy. In truth they harden us in enmity against world-spirit, which could also be called the spirit that is god as creator. However since god, as truth or world-spirit, is essentially merciful good spirit, it appears that by our continual reaction to the understandably painful and often inconvenient challenges to our selfish egos, we are not doing ourselves good but we are harming ourselves. There are degrees of the harm we can do ourselves. Arguably the least harm we can do ourselves in this sense is by socializing, exclusively with those we like, with those who are like us. They will not even mention it if we commit a faux pas. We tacitly promise not to mention their slips of etiquette either. If we are emotionally and logically sufficiently enfeebled, we may succeed in remaining socially secure against potential challenges to our egocentricity for quite some time. Be sure to be nice, make no demands and never take umbrage. Our enemy is anyone who asks an annoying question or who refuses to blank out his 'dirty emotions'. If we are lucky we sooner or later get a wake-up call, for we have stopped growing.

At the other end of the spectrum, the most unfortunate mistake we can make as we resist facing up to the challenges of our selfhood is to become part of a nation. Whether we participate, however jubilantly, in the so-called birth of 'our' nation or else support the survival of a nation to which we, however intentionally, belong, our humanity is seriously at risk. Good spirit unavoidably influences but cannot force us to welcome it. When our individualist independence and eagerness for supremacy is painfully challenged, this is then our own business. We ourselves are responsible for the pain; for the fear, the guilt and the shame. Merciful good spirit not only does not punish us – as goes with the name – but equally it does not – really because it cannot – interfere in our self-destructive behaviour. The cry: Oh Lord, punish my enemies! Must surely be seen to be absurd.

*

So world-spirit is good influence on us all at all time. *The world* however, as we commonly think of it, is not good-spiritual but a myth. We can usefully think of it as the sum-total of all reactions, our own included, to god plus all reactions to those reactions, and so on. Any attempt to change *the world* to the good would therefore be a case of replacing some of those reactions to mythic enemies by good responses to world spirit.

For example we might identify what we mean by Society as a complex of reactions to world-spirit in terms of the fear of being alone for a time. We would then do our best to identify such fear of tedium, monotony, boredom and the like in ourselves and instead of reacting to it by means of some social diversion we would seek to respond to it this time, patiently and courageously within ourselves as to a calling-card of good spirit. The intention to do so – and this is crucial – would, in good time and in fact, supply us with a particular way or manner of responding. We might, for example, find ourselves inwardly

3

with real joy. Or we might make a loving observation to our spouse. Or we might feel moved to pass our sudden good cheer on to some unhappy person in our vicinity. Or we might write a poem. The number of possibilities of how we might gain from responding (intending to respond) to a good spirit challenge to which we have made a bad habit of reacting is endless.

What I have written here contains my version of the secret of 'how to improve *the world*'.[1]

*

The world is tremendously under pressure always due to the fact that it amounts to a continuous more or less organized and systematized defence against world-spirit. This pressure plays itself out any- and everywhere as conflict. Whether in the home, on the streets or on battle fields, the agony of this conflict invites us to life and love. Wherever and however we are stationed on the earth, our own contribution to our community in terms of creative responsibility will be revealed to us if we wait in the right spirit to have it revealed to us, rather than piling more reaction on reaction in ignorance and haste.

Also we might keep in mind that whenever we find we are scandalized by some aspect of *the world* or of Society, that must mean that not only have we a similar shortfall within ourselves but, more importantly, we have what it takes to remedy matters; otherwise we would not have been scandalized. This is how our various opportunities for doing good are brought home to us, so that we might succeed. That man who is annoyed by an evil, criticizes and moves on – or worse, attacks that evil to remove it – is misguided and endangers his humanity – if he has any to begin with. If an evil angers us, quickly let

---

[1] So world spirit is neither responsible for the world nor is it somehow the effect the world has on us. We ourselves produce <u>the</u> world by resisting world spirit.

us ask ourselves how we ourselves might commit just such an evil, and then let us hope to have the corresponding good revealed to us, so that we might do it.

*

Another way of referring to reaction to world-spirit is attachment to *the world*. As soon as we refer to *the world* we mean a myth. *The world* is a myth inasmuch as we help to bring it about by reacting to world-spirit and by contradicting and resisting world-spirit when we would be smart to cooperate. By helping to bring more of *the world* about and by behaving as though it were real we distance ourselves from world-spirit.

However how can we cooperate with world-spirit if we cannot help but react to it initially?

This thought transports us into the vicinity of another secret that is well worth taking to heart, namely that we are not to turn into independent, self-sustaining individualists but that we are to be communal. Consequently in order to have our own reaction to world-spirit undone and reversed, we must undo and reverse the results of reaction in those around us. This is of course called forgiveness. We see how those around us too are under the conflictive pressure of their reactions to world-spirit and we have the choice of condemning them, thereby condemning ourselves, or of forgiving, thereby releasing ourselves. This strikes me as an interesting arrangement – and an admirable one, if the overall purpose is to create communities of human beings that love and cherish one another. Merely forgiving *ourselves*, by the way, which some people consider to be possible and worthwhile, simply locks us into ourselves. This is not recommended. It is only another reaction to an aspect of world-spirit, namely to the need to forgive others if we ourselves are to be forgiven. Instead of trying to forgive ourselves we can just stop trying to be idealists and perfectionists, and that takes care of that strange guilt at having 'messed up

5

again', i.e. not having performed to our own individualist standards. Truth is the master and we cannot improve on it. Forgiving so as to be forgiven, like being merciful so as to be worthy of mercy, is the same as furthering the humanity in others in order to invest in our own humanity.

I am presenting this so rationally and in such a logical manner because that is how nationality and politics are customarily presented, and I am trying to make some sense of what might be a useful response to such phenomena. We need to be clear about the basis of human relationship in comparison to popular 'bonding and disbanding', for the lack of a better word at present. In speaking about those who call truth falsehood and falsehood truth we do well to choose our words carefully. Those who are in favour of nationality as an end-product of sorts will of course insist that their arguments are rational and logical, however it is plainly a mythic, self-produced rationality and logic and if we are to get anywhere we have to let that pass.

Up to us to learn how to identify the initial reactivity to the creator world-spirit, so that we can grow into another good habit, every time, of responsiveness and true responsibility. Up to us to identify correctly the reactionary behaviour of others and to learn how to forgive, how to love unconditionally, how to be merciful – otherwise we are bound to become involved in such behaviour, either by falling in with it or by resisting it.

*

The logic of judging the behaviour of others is faulty. We may find the decisions made by our democratic representatives wise or obscene, however these people are as worthy of respect as anyone else. Treating people disrespectfully makes them more likely to behave reactively. So surely a climate of respect for politicians has to be created from the start, otherwise there can be no communication. Such respect is a form of love and must therefore be unconditional, not based on the politician's

6

behaviour. Does unconditional human respect cause us to view people through rose-coloured glasses? On the contrary. It clears our mind of prejudice, we rise to a more enlightened point of view and we help someone overcome his moral handicaps creatively because we call to mind our own vulnerability.

Moralizing is not creative. When we moralize we usually speak as if we ourselves were good. No one is good and criticism is not creative. When we criticize we pretend to be beyond any temptation. Creativity, on the other hand, can be usefully described as our growing along compassionately with the one we encourage to grow. When someone is stuck in a state of being, our compassion for that person prompts us to recall how we ourselves get stuck at times and now, in community with him, we may overcome any hindrance to growth – which hindrance, by the way, does not even need to be identified. That is how love, and any form of love such as respect, works. The last thing in our mind is to seek recognition for what we have achieved, since love has achieved it, and the loving we do necessarily proceeds in cooperation with the source of love, which is merciful good spirit and – more aptly in our present case, creative world-spirit.

If we want to do good, let us aim it at persons, not at policies. One aim of love and of doing good is to facilitate growth, towards and in maturity. Along with moral and ethical maturity can come evolutionary breakthrough into the realm of spiritual reality; now and again this happens. Thereafter one finds oneself in a position from where one is capable of genuinely good influence. Such influence then arises from one's being, one's behaving, doing and acting. Also one automatically considers oneself to be on the earth for some certain good purpose. Certainly one always wishes there were more who were at home in spiritual reality and it makes reasonable good sense to hope for that. Meanwhile one aims to help others, of whatever age, towards maturity or to greater maturity. In that way one grows in wisdom oneself.

*

Those who espouse popular reality and seek to be first, like to lord it over others. Those who feel urged to be first in spiritual reality are wise to seek to be least. They are here and now not for themselves but for others.

From the point of view of spiritual reality it is nonetheless possible to speak of country, of citizenship, of government in a way that urges the popular mind in the direction of honourable behaviour. Such behaviour overcomes anxiety and distress. It furthers a sense of worth and encourages participation in government. Sometimes the greatest scoundrels rise to the top on a tide of those who have ceased to care for their humanity. Even such a deplorable situation can be turned around by those who behave honourably and take an interest in government.

In spiritual reality we all govern ourselves. We know government from within. Therefore we can guide those who need to be governed from the outside, who can not yet function properly in the absence of rules, regulations and laws.

I stress the development of a sense of honour. No one can learn in a spirit of arrogance or of servility. Schools that enslave the human spirit in the interest of servitude to the state should be closed and replaced by academies where children can learn to feel and think at the same time, rather than separating the intellect from the will in order to manufacture pliable cogs in the State-machinery. Once a nation is set on its course, there is no holding it. Every attempt to change the course of national development is self-defeating. Fools cry: We want to be a nation. We want to be a nation again. We want our nation to be great again! We want to influence *the world*, to be strong enough to impose our will! – What has that to do with govern-

8

ment? A nation by definition needs itself to be governed and this task is taken in hand, if I may put it that way, by unavoidable circumstances and unalterable conditions. Whatever is born and then not raised from among the dead must die. It has no control over itself, though it may fool itself that it does.

It should be possible for any segment of population that has espoused nationhood also to divest itself of nationhood. Nations nowadays reek of fear. They cannot think past the enemy, imagined or ideal, that has it in for them. They are either enslaved by their past or set on some libertarian collision course with an uncertain future. Who can still think rationally about the obscenity of competitive stockpiling of nuclear weaponry![1] How readily is it not accepted that heads of government will be hounded out of office if they give in to their better nature! How often do we not wonder do they actually have one?

However we become our worst enemies when we get caught up in a mechanism that seemed to promise some meaningful scope for our abundant energy and suddenly it has turned into a straitjacket.

So with modern nationhood. We live in a time now when all that is hidden is revealed if it is the least bit worth knowing for those who take the next few steps up the evolution-ladder. How fine it would be to be able to live in a *country* again, not in a nation, but this time where honest words are spoken and no one is afraid to let his human essence shine through! The extinction of the nation-concept holds few surprises for most of the population, who never could warm to it in the first place. Professional careerists will not understand that their time is up; a *country* does not need to be 'run'; not even like a competitive business. A certain type of individual who has no connection

---

[1] See the work of Martin Hellman, American cryptologist who takes a keen interest in world affairs, the avoidance of nuclear war, the efficacy of unconditional love, etc.

with the ethos of the population is no longer needed. No doubt others will come forward, not afraid to minister in the true sense of that word. Then we will be able to burn bombs, to turn swords into ploughshares. Is that pie in the sky? We shall see.

*

Who and what, then, is the real enemy of the nations?

We notice that every defensive move by a nation, nowadays, is interpreted as an offensive move by another nation, who then feels justified to defend itself again, which is perceived as a further offense. Seemingly intelligent, well-meaning men and women are voted democratically into office, only to commence with the behaviour one would expect from an ill-bred individual – and the population goes along with this. The population – of a nation now – to all intents and purposes seems, in the end, to be powerless when one supposes it should be overseeing, in the strictest sense, what those who allegedly represent it and who are in a position to minister to it often do instead, namely engage in acts, on their behalf no less, that would by themselves in their everyday lives be readily understood as ego-centric and selfish.

To the extent that the spirit of *country* and land is also active in a nation, a lively contest exists between those who interpret self-government in the national idiom and those who experience it on a daily basis in a personal sense. So what I mean by a *country* or land in comparison to a nation depends on the meaning of liberty which, by those who despair of the national spirit, is seen as an inherent right and experienced as a possession which cannot be taken from them, so that when those who abide by the national spirit would oblige and even obligate them by handing them liberty, as a gift from the angels as it were, they balk and feel dishonoured. What we see next then, clearly in our time, is that famous 'disconnect' between those who govern in terms of national and nationalist ideas, who are suddenly confused, and those who feel unaddressed, misunderstood and disaffected. The national rulers cannot understand why their very best efforts are not universally appreciated. Imagine if someone were to tell you that you have to find a way to justify your humanity before you will benefit from what he is willing to give only to human beings. When you ask what he is willing to give, he says 'your liberty'. All depends now on how long and how thoroughly you have been indoctrinated in the idealism and ideology of the political state before it occurs to you to think: Hold on, as a human being I am at liberty.

In truth, I repeat, the political state or nation is not a good thing. Essentially it is imposed and can only be perceived by the human spirit as an imposition. No use blaming those who impose it. No use either trying to depose them. Their acquired predisposition to ideal thinking and idealist feeling can only be challenged by themselves. It remains for those who adhere to an ethic of down-to-earth practicality to prove their worth – not as leaders but as exemplary *countrymen* and *countrywomen* who are willing to help out in times of need.

One looks forward to their arrival on the stage of the commonweal.

*

One useful comparison to any nation is a particular human household. In terms of a State or Nation, however, one speaks of the economy and one encourages the 'growth of the economy'. What I mean by a household is not an idea but down-to-earth reality. There is no reason why the household of the land should be managed any differently from the household of a family or even of an individual person.

The economy of the nation is dangled before us as something that must forever grow and this growth is not organic but mathematical. As a consequence the population is under duress and may even feel obliged to increase consumption. This is a basic factor by which a nation seeks to perpetuate itself. The idea of surviving within one's means does not exist and is not allowed to exist because it would undermine the anxiety-based desire for 'progress'.

A critique of the nation and of the nation state must begin from the premise that nationality is a modern invention and therefore rigged in terms of anxious survival. Real life, eternal life, cannot be allowed to come into it but must be disparaged and ridiculed. Slightly with tongue in cheek we might come to the peculiar conclusion that the nation is really a racist establishment because the human race is not allowed to come to the fore. Enough said that individual human households, which thrive as adjuncts to life, help us to survive not anxiously, stretched between fear of scarcity and conspicuous consumption, but within our means and therefore they make for a restful existence.

Not that those who really live must struggle to protect themselves against contamination by the modern, anxiety-riddled life. No, modern life insists on itself and to that degree it diminishes. Those who live the contemporary, real life are too busy minding their own restful business to concern themselves, except compassionately, over those who make a career of the modern anxiety-avoidance and will therefore never have enough energy to go around – and misperceived scarcity of energy is the cause of all wars.

*

Living within one's means is the art of all arts. One begins with the notion that availability of supply is given. In terms of mere survival, that is of survival itself as life, this would be an absurd idea. The modern individual cannot begin to live until his stomach is full. He points to the hordes of the hungry poor

12

to bolster his argument. However there is no arguing with him because he is ruled by the idea of the necessity to survive.

The home and the household are destroyed by that idea. I suppose we eventually have to begin with the perhaps somewhat outdated notion that if we live well there will be no shortage of supply. What do I mean by living well? To begin with I assume that where I am placed on the earth, which includes the country I live in and any country to which I am shifted by circumstances beyond my control, is most suitable for me if I want to learn how to live well, in a home, managing a household. I stress the importance of native awareness. The idea of circumstances beyond one's control causes the member of a nationally inclined society serious trepidation because he is taught from young – he is conditioned to believe – that a man is not responsible for himself so much as for his conditions.

This introduces us to the worthwhile notion that a real home is not really a condition or set of conditions that we more or less strenuously bring about but it develops and grows over time. Ideas of self-conditioning, as a consequence, have to be rejected as interference with the spontaneity that steadily succeeds careful planning within present and available means.

It is after all what spontaneously happens that makes us happy; not what happens accidentally, but spontaneously and unforeseeably. And there must be careful planning; but planning within contemporary means. So it does not count as careful planning if we set out to accumulate as much money as possible so that we can purchase what we suppose will make us happy. We cannot know what thing will make us happy, that is the long and the short of it.

What I mean by careful planning, for one example, is that we begin with what is at hand, not with what lies on the opposite side of the mountain. Means at our disposal are therefore valued in line with how well we can fit them into our careful plans. I use the word care here the way a human being would use it, in other words care as a demonstration or enactment of unconditional love. Careful planning, which sees to immediate needs, takes the fullest possible advantage of all that happens spontaneously in the meanwhile – always keeping in mind that spontaneity is neither accidental nor lucky. It succeeds sufficient planning – that is to say, sufficient for spontaneity to be able to set in. Any direct results of our planning really only interest us peripherally. We plan with a feather-light touch. So for example I may plan to make the furniture for our spare room. I draw up a few designs and count the cost when suddenly a complete set of perfectly suitable furniture falls into my lap and all I have to do is say thank you. It would not occur to me now to maintain that the preparation was useless. I personally began with nothing but now live in a comfortable home in which my wife and I have raised three children and I cannot take credit for much of it – except perhaps for the fact that we always lived strictly within our means. We accepted help when it was offered, consumed frugally and wasted as little as possible.

We can speak about planned spontaneity but we all have to discover for ourselves the open secret that is implied.

*

Planning, maintaining order, repairing right away what is broken, handling belongings with care, accepting help from neighbours and offering help to them, planting a garden and sharing the surplus, making extra jam to be used as gifts, using whatever money comes in wisely and always saving up for the next purchase, whether it's a second-hand car or a new refrigerator – and so on. Can a country not be maintained like this? There is no mention of an enemy. There is no boasting about being more influential in *the world* than some other *country*.

There is no need for secrets, for a Secret Service. All service is out in the open. An army would create enemies.

Aha! you say, there's the rub. A neighbouring State would swallow you up. You have to be able to defend yourself. Really? Is the USA at the moment able to defend itself against Russia or China? Are they able to defend themselves against the USA? Not even against North Korea does a reasonable defence seem feasible. Nothing but a tense half-peace exists. Nations are doomed by their own inventiveness. Any rational relation or even contact between national governments and the citizenry appears unworkable over any appreciable period of time. Is the ship of State not breaking up on the reefs? Is it not too late for patching and painting?

Nor can I see any sense in trying to make the craft seaworthy again. It never has been seaworthy. It was a raft on which refugees from their own faulty state-craft sailed into the supernatural blue distance, hoping against hope that this time the experiment would take root and thrive.

However all the mixing of metaphors in the world will not help me persuade those who are sold on the idea of the 'most powerful nation in the world that can always be fixed'. My plea goes out to those who create a home in a *country*. This can go on even while the Nation State still limps along, leaning on its stock-exchange and realizing it hasn't a friend in the world because its gestures are misleading and its speech is not truthful.

Making a home in a *country* – there lies the future. A handful of creative human beings can start the ball rolling.

Do I choose to behave and think like a citizen in the United States of America or like a free human being in the *country* called America? Do I see myself as subject to a Queen in the conditional monarchy called Great Britain or as a free human being in England, Wales, Scotland or Northern Ireland, think-

15

ing of them as *countries*? How frightened the citizens and the subjects are when the human beings defect! Why not put them at their ease? They have everything to gain. Political power is a Chimaera. The only power we have is for the good we can do in the interest of human being and human life.

*

Creating a home and a *country*, if necessary even within a nation, that is the task we face. Even if we decide that the nation is evil – we do not resist evil. Give to Caesar what is Caesar's. We quietly get together and pool our spiritual resources. We do not form clubs, denominations, societies, organizations, institutions, etc. We do not even form communities because any worthwhile community forms itself in time and is never externally recognizable. We are free men and women and children. Our freedom is real, spiritual. Even if someone should choose to incarcerate us, he cannot take our freedom from us because it grows out of the liberty with which we were born. So sad, all these attempts to manufacture liberty, when liberty waits to be recognized and acknowledged by each of us within ourselves.

It sounds familiar, this. We have heard it so often. Have we, though? For one example, we do not interfere with the State, we just know it for what it is, namely a mythic creation that externalizes for us our worst intentions and possibilities. The nation mirrors the individual. An individual is not a person. An individual (why do we never ask: an individual what?) has no personality and is not a person. What is it that personality changes about an individual, turning him/into an individual person or a person with individuality? In other words, what is the difference between an individual and a person? Is it self-expression? Well, strictly now, an individual does express his self. A person, by comparison, offers his/her human being. That is quite a difference, however it does not quite get at the crux of the matter. If we want to talk about home and *country*, which is our chosen formula for the moment, we have to look at willingness, intention and ability to love unconditionally, which implies that we are always loved and that we prefer to love, especially at times when we feel like doing the opposite, which happens often enough when we are not looking.

How are we always loved? By good spirit, which creates us and loves us. Or put it the other way: Good spirit is the love that always influences us, whether we like it or not. To the extent that we resist this love we become conscious of hatred in ourselves and have the choice of indulging ourself in it, as individuals – or of loving instead, as persons. Good spirit is not evil, nor does it cause evil. We, by ignoring it, become involved in evil and by negating this spirit we do what is evil.

Good spirit, then, is the spirit in which we create home and *country*.

*

The word 'home' means a lot to me. It took me a long time to 'go home', so no wonder that I see a difference between my spiritual home, which is my immediate inward being, and the home I live in, which I make. It may be a house, though it can also be a tent, a caravan, a shelter in the woods, that sort of thing.

If I were not spiritually at home, how could I make a home? I could not. My spiritual home I take with me wherever I go. Also it doesn't take me long to 'make myself at home' when, for example, I go on holiday to Crete, although, truth to tell, my wife does most of it for both of us. She draws on her own spiritual home meanwhile. It's not that much different from my own. In fact the two merge to a great extent.

17

However we are not 'stay-at-homes'. We both work, so we go out from our made home and come back to it, never intentionally leaving our spiritual home,

Our spiritual, real home is not private. Nor is our made home public. 'Private' and 'public' do not apply. Still, it stands to reason that one does not invite just anyone into one's home, made or spiritual.

Is the made home not real? Of course it is, however only to the degree that it reflects the spiritual home. When you visit someone in their (made) home you can soon tell whether those who live there are spiritually mature or more or less hunted out of themselves by the modern spirit of progress. I certainly know first hand what that is like.

Human beings like to work and their work invariably does take them into areas of – shall we call it 'lesser spiritual maturity'. That means we do well to go home again, to reconnect to the source of what is good for us. We want to grow, don't we, as human beings. We really cannot afford to concern ourselves overly with those who insist on taking no account of their spiritual, real home. Perhaps the example we set and the work we do will trigger a response from them, who can say. Hope springs eternal.

Well, when I think about this place where I live, there is this and that about it that makes good sense to me. There is also this and that which appears to me to be nonsense. That much being given, I might ask myself now how I can help to shape this as a *country,* sensibly. How, for example do I talk about it to others? What sort of interest do I take in it, in its history, for example and especially in those who have helped to shape it to become what it is today? This interest will not amount to a vicarious gathering of information, but always I will look for those aspects of my *country* that touch me personally and correspond to my sense of my spiritual home. Quite possibly I

18

have a lot of work cut out for me. All the same I will know I am doing something important. Little by little my own sense of *country* develops. More and more correspondences will rise to the surface. The work I do may help or hinder how I see my *country*, so that bears looking at. I may live on a farm, in a village, a town or a city. My initial responsibility rests, of course, with the closer, more intimate surroundings and as I engage in this or that activity I make my presence felt, as I behave respectfully and honourably, depending on my rank. My influence on my environment may be predominantly moral, ethical, religious or spiritual. This has to do with who I am and how I see myself in terms of my god.

Or let me put it this way: Even if I were to live in 'the most powerful nation on the earth' – and we know what sort of power that is – I would try to create a sense of *country* and to influence others in that sense, rather than falling in with national predispositions or participating in nationalistic concerns. After all I am not an individual. Nor am I, worse, an individualist (corresponding to national and nationalist) but a spiritual person and an individual human being. Especially how I think and feel, how I talk and what I say will create that influential sense of *country*, which others may well imitate or adopt. Quite possibly it will seem more real, more down to earth to them than what they have considered so far.

*

If an individual is to raise himself, developmentally, out of his self-absorption, will it help him to band together with a group, or even a crowd, of self-absorbed individuals? Will that help his development towards personality and mature communication? Whether we are individuals because of arrested development or on account of a lack of moral stamina, that makes no difference. What counts is that every individual should take upon himself the burden of change so that he may learn to carry it in his or her own individual way. Individuality is not crowd mentality. Due to our individuality we are unique in the way we move forward and up to personal community, each making his own singular contribution. That makes for live and lively world experience. We are not, on the other hand, individual so as to agree with other individuals on the method by which we might succeed in continuing to be individuals. However only those who themselves value maturity will see the absurdity in this.

By clinging together, we individuals set ourselves up for a much, much bigger shock than the one that would have educated us, as single individuals, out of our self-complacency and out of our dangerous arrogance.

*

When a population within borders declares itself in favour of forming itself as a nation state, this is a collective effort by many individuals to justify their self-complacency and their arrogance. It is always an attempt to blind oneself to one's individual responsibility by drowning it in a great pool, in a mass, of irresponsible individuals. A nation state only works – only seems to work – until the moment arrives of the big wake-up call.

As a member of a nation state, an individual may continue for a while to practice self-complacency and/or arrogance. Nations are made by us, they do not come into being magically.

So just as a human individual may wake up to the fact that his individualism cannot be the end of a beautiful story, so too may a nation be understood as something out of which and beyond which we have to move if we are to avoid the greatest wake-up call of all today. The nation-state is collective individualism, whether out of complacency or from a hunger for might; these two augment each other and play into each other.

20

Individualism, rather than individual personality, is a dangerous game to play and when nations play it there is wholesale destruction and bloodshed to come – perhaps after a period of somnolence or lethargy. However when nations band together into a kind of super-state, hoping thereby to cure themselves of the national arrogance, then this is not different from individuals banding together as a nation. It is self-complacency and arrogance to a higher power.

The way for a nation to grow up is not by joining other nations but by becoming a *country*. What I call *country* is to nation state as person is to individualism. To a convinced individual, the suggestion of personhood is bound to sound, at first, as an absurdity. We make hard and fast habits and routines out of our individualism and we rightly sense that any change away from our cherished illusion of normality is bound to be somewhat painful. However the pain will be in inverse proportion to the degree of our knowledge and understanding of our human nature, our nature not only as potentially productive but also as urge to our maturity as personal human beings

So too will a population not readily take to the *country*-mentality. Dissatisfaction with unavoidable national competition can, however, be a good start, especially since war nowadays must be seen as an obscenity, in the light of the possible total destruction of civilized life on earth. Very likely a more hands-on democracy will be created, where the time is taken to arrive at consensus. Certainly hardened individuals are best served by exemplary acceptance, not by exclusion. What I mean by *country* will gradually eclipse such ideas as nation, state, earthly kingdom and empire.

Once this difference between the notion of *country* and the idea of nation is somewhat understood, one will shape one's decisions piecemeal, over time, one at a time in the direction of rational humanity. One will learn to think in terms of men, women and children, of concrete improvements to life-style and quality of life, rather than in terms of puerile one-upmanship and political role-play.

Individuality is the name we give to our uniqueness as we hope to achieve spiritual maturity. We can only really develop in our own individual way. An individual, by comparison, has no interest in personal growth and development. However to the extent that we become personally effective our individuality continues unhindered.

*

So should we also be able to speak of something like the personal individuality of a *country*? Even states like France, Germany, England and Ireland have a character of their own, even a personality, if you like, which is the obvious reflection, past and present, of Frenchmen, Germans, the English and the Irish. And character is not developed by guarding against difference, against the stranger, but by welcoming every challenge to one's identity and one's security in oneself. Forget about existing in peace and harmony and learn to live productively and creatively in community. What we do to avoid war brings on war. Idealism favours resistance of evil and so multiplies evil. Doing down-to-earth good can be a full-time occupation and those who insist on impersonal individualism will be won over sooner or later.

The very concept of 'the most powerful nation on earth' makes human beings ashamed of themselves for being part of it. Do we, ordinarily, like bullies? I don't think so. In that case, why would we want our nation to beat up other nations? Well, only silly people do that. All the same, there must be many, because if there were not, how would professional politicians dare to behave as they do? Do they know something about the population of our country that we don't know? Are they catering to the lowest common denominator?

I think of Northern Ireland (where I live) as a model *country* – in the making. (That seems reminiscent of Hegel in Prussia, but what a difference!) Hardly anyone has heard of Northern Ireland and that's a good sign. Everything about this piece of geography is difficult. First of all, part of the South (Eira) is further north. Then, part of the province of Ulster is in the South. The struggle against the nation called Eire, the South, the Republic, is no longer what it was because the South is becoming less nationalistic, as I see it, and the North is more and more able to think of itself as an organic unit and not just a bit of self-interest against this, that and the other thing. (One quarter of the two million population is concentrated in Belfast.)

The feel of this place is friendly though the big city is of course a bit of an impersonal experience, as you would expect. After all we are part and parcel of a kingdom, though you'd hardly notice. So we have a kingdom on one side and a sovereign state on the other. One question that keeps popping up in my mind is: Are there only the two choices for us, namely British or part of an all-Ireland? What about the *country* of Northern Ireland?

Oh good heavens! I hear the chorus: Northern Ireland could never support itself. Is that not a matter of opinion? I agree, as an independent state Northern Ireland makes no sense. However as a *country* among – well, eventually among other *countries*, does that still sound ridiculous? In a lively community you come across rich and poor, professional and lay; also black, white, brown and yellow skin colour. Then there is the geography, the weather and the climate. Also, by definition, (as I define it) a *country* is not in survival-competition with other *countries*. We have to posit a degree of collective decency here and the people of Northern Ireland are, by and large, a decent and industrious people. They also like to be creative. A few opposite influences come together and that is fruitful, because you have to be creative to overcome hindrances to your growth.

Surely *countries* come into being because sensible people want to cooperate. They can also come about when kingdoms break up and nations break down. When a nation begins to deplore the idea of its standing in *the world* and of the role it wants to – feels it ought to – play in *the world*, it 'breaks down' and begins to think of itself as a *country*, which is progress. More to the point, the population begins to prefer cooperation to status. Kingdoms are liable to break up when portions of it develop a healthy sense of authenticity (Scotland). After the British Empire broke up, its various colonies grew strong. – However these are mere indications.

It is such a different type of thinking that goes on when a population concentrates on itself and discovers both originality and authenticity. Certainly *countries* are not drawn up on a map, like some middle eastern countries after a war. They are not decided on from outside. And the central impulse is not selfish independence but generous pride.

I have a vision of the earth's surface populated by a thousand and one *countries*, all getting along like sensible, decent people do. No global policeman is necessary. The ethic of friendship will eventually be paramount. Remember that a *country* has no leaders who decide what is good for it and no politicians who make a carer of swaying people's minds in some direction. How can a *country* get on without representatives, elected or otherwise? People will find ways of speaking for themselves. The only reason why democracy is not considered to be too old-fashioned is that alternatives are usually even less appropriate in an inter-national environment. It won't be long before there is no longer a USA, a Russia or a China. The next hundred years will decide it.

The super-nation-states will not disarm until they break up. They behave like ill-brought up children, each accusing the other of its own shortcomings and suspecting the other of its own vices. Something new, different and better is in the air and I look forward to it.

*

With this nuclear stalemate upon us, I ask myself once again how is this different from the case of individual persons, once they see themselves as true human beings and realize they cannot possibly harm or hurt anyone without hurting and harming themselves? Accidents will happen of course and then we apologize and make up for it as best we can. So-called nuclear nations find themselves in the same situation. They sit poised at the ready, with arsenals stocked, able to over-kill. Except that an accident may well leave no one alive to apologize or to apologize to.

Now human beings, once they realize they cannot harm with impunity because the human spirit crosses the individual barriers, do not settle for a harmless life. They will never be satisfied with the ethic of harmlessness, of general peace and quiet. Why not? There is no growth in it; no development, no evolution. The harmless life is decadent. So they reach out. What else is non-resistance of evil and love of enemy in combination but heaping gifts on one another and serving and ministering to one another? Especially to those who dislike us, who hate us! Is that too much to ask of a country? I fear that all else will amount to pious sentiments and empty words and gestures.

It would take someone with a little creative imagination to study that enemy nation, to understand its fears, to address them tangibly and not make a big thing out of it. It would be the exact moral opposite of insisting that those people adopt our ideology. We would find clever ways of anticipating certain needs and helping to satisfy them. That sort of positive action, I am convinced, would work to renew trust, when nothing else does. Remove those missiles from Turkey, but don't do it so that Russia will remove theirs from Cuba. No, do it because you have decided it is the right thing to do and a good action. Halt US and South Korea military exercises not to get North Korea to halt its missile testing but because those exercises are a bad thing and stopping them is good. Only what is done in good spirit bears good fruit.

I deal with pain like that, both mental and physical pain. I suffer it, not so that it goes away but so that I can continue to grow. I understand, after all, that I am responsible for the pain in the first place. Somehow I have caused a blockage. Somehow we are responsible for those Russian nuclear arms. What they do with theirs now is their business. When there is no more need for them, and considering how much it costs to keep them, what do we expect they will do?

And what about that poor beleaguered man in North Korea? Why not congratulate him on his new missile launch? Well done, Mr. Kindly Leader. – The old way of thinking: That will only encourage him to launch more of them. The new and better way: It eases the tension for him. He is modern and congenitally anxious like ourselves. All those rockets, those nuclear war-heads, whoever owns them or tests them, are pure expressions of modern anxiety. Faith, honesty, trust, love. All unconditionally extended. Miracles will happen, wait till you see. Old men around a forum table cannot even imagine such behaviour, not to mention acting it out.

And if we ever do set out, energetically and imaginatively, on the road to friendship by extending the hand to the enemy, we will have our answers ready for those who still only know tit for tat, an eye for an eye, keep the other guy guessing and steal his sheep when he's not looking. We will patiently explain the new thinking to them and maybe enrol them in the good work.

Do we have to be moral giants nowadays before we can behave magnanimously? At some time in the past, war may have included an honourable element. Nowadays cowards wage a petty, obscene war, akin to mass murder, and you don't ever even look the enemy in the eye. You mostly 'take him out' from a distance. He's a thing.

*

The typical modern anxiety that is in us all whether we like it and are aware of it or not, needs to be faced, to be dealt with. I have written elsewhere about the metaphysical cause and origin of that anxiety. The anxiety itself is closely tied into our native liberty to do as we please. Millions upon millions of people on the earth cannot fathom how it should be that they experience liberty as their inheritance while at the same time their anxiety either gets them into trouble, outside in *the world*, or inside as a psyche, as depression or mania.

So while we want to be understood by those millions – I mean those who are liable to be led or misled because their opinions remain unstructured and do not develop into thought – we do well not to speak of causes of the anxiety, as if one could remove it and leave their psyche somehow healed. No, the psyche is this anxiety and when magicians and sorcerers momentarily trick the anxiety, the psyche, away (empty rhetoric, charisma in poetry, in music) what is left is a big hole, a nothing. Nihilism, like atheism or religious fundamentalism, disports itself for a time in that 'nothing' but then it vacates the premises just shortly before the unavoidable collapse.

Millions make it difficult for those who represent them politically to act on the basis of ethical thought – like the bride who married the groom because he promised to make her happy – big mistake! Nobody can do that. "Look, love, I'm sorry, I promised too much, but maybe we could consider how to become responsible for ourselves like mature adults." So does the politician have to tell a pack of lies to get into 'power' so that he can then behave and act truthfully? Halfway he is there already.

*

So let us not get involved in any discussions with the millions about what causes the modern, pervasive anxiety. Let's not even bother to disagree with those who blame bad food, not enough sex or the influx of foreigners into our innocent country. No need to bother with that because a.) we know that the anxiety is actually in itself an invitation to the banquet and b.) we have, up our sleeve, quite a few suggestions as to how to accept that invitation.

Now if that is not new thinking, I don't know what is.

The anxiety manifests itself in a million and one ways. For example, it makes us suppose that someone has harmed us, or could harm us, and so we hang a sign around his neck: ENEMY! Whereupon this anxiety persuades us that we either should kill that ENEMY or protect ourselves against him, by hook or by crook; by club, bow and arrow or by intercontinental ballistic missiles.

Mercy me! Is that how it works?

That's how it works – for but one instance.

Is the anxiety to blame? Not at all. The anxiety is the invitation to the banquet – let's, for the sake of the argument, call it the banquet of the global community. The word 'global' has a certain 'pull' these days (as if one could not just as readily be globally selfish!)

So instead of resisting that anxiety, whenever it lights up in us, and structuring a system of animosity, and possibly building a National Defense System in fear of 'the first strike' (how puerile is that!) or so as to be able to deal with that 'rogue state' (how arrogant is that!) we sit down for a moment and check with our humanity, our gifted human nature, and lo and behold! we come up, the two or three of us, with the most common-sensical and beautiful notions that are magnanimous and imaginative and creative, and where did they come from? And where is that anxiety?

What anxiety? Let the banquet begin.

*

So we can draw a straight line from that unavoidable modern anxiety to the banquet that stands for the world community. What's that you say? You're not anxious? You don't know what I'm talking about? You have no enemies? Never? Then I'd love to hear from you. I'm always ready to learn. Are you married? And you never have an enemy? What about the Russians, the Jews, the Chinese, the Palestinians, or that "black bastard who stole my convertible and wrecked it" – aha, you see, I heard you at the time, it was a week or so before 9/11. For my sake too, think again. How safe are you in our nuclear age, so called?

I may be wasting my time here.

Another form of the somehow unignorable modern anxiety is the indifference bordering on psychosis, the enervation, the lethargy that sets in when people give up trying to understand.

The anxiety, if we pay no attention, overwhelms us. If we react to it, it undermines us. Surely that's understandable, even from what we know of our own experience during our daily life. There is anxious activity and anxious passivity. In neither case is there good action or passion. Let's not fool ourselves.

29

Due to not all but most of the drugs we take we kill the messenger who would invite us to the banquet. The negative role of the media can be heedlessly to excite us or culpably to pacify us. All the same, we are the ones who drug ourselves and who seek vicarious excitement. We ourselves are responsible.

Just a hint now: The anxiety is due to *the world* into which we were born, the world we ourselves have produced by reacting to world-spirit – we with our liberal, gifted human nature. Would you take a two-year-old child to a horror movie? That's a metaphor.

*

While we are still able to be anxious in this finite *world* there is hope for us. We may count ourselves fortunate that we are able to experience this existential anxiety, this psychic panic. There is the strait-jacket of modern life, as we know it and there is the unlimited space, the nothing, really, that brings us out in a sweat. Politically imagined, we feel the need to conquer more territory, the imperialistic drive, the cry for 'Lebensraum', as A. Schickelgruber called it – and there is the corresponding need to build a wall around ourselves, a Chinese-type wall, to keep out the Mongol hordes, the immoral Mexicans, the West-Germans, the Catholics or the Protestants, you name it, to prevent contamination due to foreign ideology. The fear of being enclosed and the need to be enclosed – how can anyone make sense of that? They are the two sides of the same, infinitely thin, coin. Viewed from within, we call it egotism and selfishness. You have to survive. You have to live. Same thing, isn't it? Is there anyone nowadays who really and truly has a choice? With sincere sorrow we view the populations of the nations and can but sympathize with their representative 'leaders' who struggle in their own straitjackets and search far and wide for walls, for materials to build those walls. What a relief for them when they come up with another enemy! What a relief for the military establishment, which is, in a pinch, glad to assist in the manufacture of enemies. No one likes to face the enemy within. He cannot be relied upon to 'stand and fight'.

Are Mrs. Permaneder's hot-flushes and panic-attacks essentially different from certain political and economical crises? I don't think so. Let those who fancy interfering humanistically on the national or international level look first to their own hot-flushes and panic-attacks; then they will be able to offer helpful advice.

Blessed are the anxious, for they shall know rest.

Do you have to do anything, in the meanwhile? Well, for one thing, relax first, before you act. But then do act. See how it looks, when you've acted. Not quite happy with it? Change your approach a little, your attitude. What motivates you – look into that – again and again. We don't learn how to do good overnight – very often. Don't fiddle with your mirror image. The nation is your mirror image. Then again, I wouldn't suggest that you break the mirror either. Did you do it already? In a fit? Due to a lack of fit? Never mind. Get a new one.

I cannot, for the life of me, get hot and bothered about the ICBM silos. I know, I know, total destruction of everything looms and I do respect those who draw my attention to it. However the forty odd years of 'new thinking' I have done and the 'quantum leap forward' I have taken were good-spiritually, not fearfully motivated. Every kingdom, nation, empire on the earth during the last two-thousand years is, however, fear-motivated, anxiety-based – and therefore ill-based. I'm so sorry but that's true. I wish it were otherwise.

It's a hard truth to face for many, but no amount of fearful concentration on survival opens the door to life. Once we concentrate on living, the survival moves into second place and the anxiety diminishes. It has always been 'old thinking' that you have to survive to be able to live. The 'old thinking' is as deeply ingrained in us as that two and two make four.

Look at the political history of any nation today, at the mistrustful grouping and regrouping of alliances, treaties formed and broken, more armed conflict – then maybe someone comes along like F. Hegel with a tricky mechanism in a silver box and he says: "We have arrived! I am the truth! Prussia is the heavenly kingdom on earth!" Napoleon B. hears that and says: "Hold on a minute! What about me? I would like to create a political state based on my own internal and private predilections and trepidations." Once again the people have a reason to survive. Hitler gave the poor Germans another reason to survive. It was a feeling. Survival can sometimes be nothing but an emotion. Then the corpses are counted. Then the dead are celebrated. They have given their lives (sorry, their survival) for the nation. Don't think about it. It's too painful.

*

The simple truth again is: If we don't let merciful good spirit of love govern us, which is most human-natural, then we expose ourselves to outside forces such as empires, kingdoms, nations and states. If we cannot discipline ourselves, which is a human-natural thing to do, then we will be disciplined, which is never pleasant. Also, the 'new thinking' that is called for by those who are afraid for themselves and their civilization is, for that reason, still not founded on trust, is it. What if western civilization itself were merely a stop-gap? Far be it from me to suggest such a thing. Our citizens are so much wiser than the Iraqis, Afghans, the Lebanese, etc. who rejected our combined efforts to civilize them. We removed their bad leaders and laid democracy in their laps and before long they were fighting among themselves. "Why can't they be like we *are*, perfect in every way!"

In a *country,* those whose word is respected will not take bribes, that goes without saying. Also they will refrain from taking bribes and such not from fear of being found out but because they are aware of the life-furthering effects of honourable behaviour. They will concentrate on living – morally, ethically, respectfully, religiously, honourably – there are so many ways to live well – and as a consequence they will survive – almost absent-mindedly. The living and the surviving will go hand in hand for some. Others will live first and survival will fall in their laps.

We should not pretend to know all there is to know about this topic of life and survival. No organizing dogma will ever be available. However we should not expect that any manipulation, however clever or imaginative, of mechanisms that have been set up to facilitate and ensure survival, will ever get us out of the present bind, where the near equivalent of professional killers rule the roost. Let us not expect that huge industries founded on the need to protect against enemies will ever agree to being dismantled because there are no more enemies out there. No, as I mentioned before, enemies will be produced and invented, for the most spurious of reasons, in spite of any amount of assurance that each of us carries his own peculiar enemy within him; we do not learn how to govern ourselves while we concentrate on resisting enemies either inside or outside of us.

Nations are constructs for the purpose of defence and in the interest of self-identification as being free from constraint. A lie, in combination with a falsehood, then gradually moves along a destructive path towards its own destruction. Freedom from constraint is not freedom at all but liberty, and since we are born at liberty, a lot of malicious gossip, professionally sanctioned, has to be popularized before we accept that our subsequent lack of liberty is not our own individual fault but the responsibility of outside forces and agencies, i.e. enemies. Freedom, to say it again, resides in individual personality in terms of creative merciful love. The signs of freedom, for those who look for signs, are decent behaviour and good works. Those who forever spot enemies outside of themselves haven't the foggiest notion of freedom. Anyway, we are given enemies to love, not to hate and fight.

The cause of every war, whatever excuse is brought forward afterwards, is always a stagnation in the human-natural growth process. Even the cupidity of the brute who intentionally overreaches himself, arises, if not from such stagnation, then from a total ignorance of such human-organic growth. Entire populations of modern nation-states are ignorant of their human-natural growth. Who can be educated – that is to say, who can be drawn out of that stagnation – so that war will not be necessary?

Or perhaps the post-modern stagnation is such that not even war can be counted on as a remedy?

The aim for human beings is life, not survival.

Is the end of survival for its own sake then therefore desuetude of the will to live?

* * * * *

www.ingramcontent.com/pod-product-compliance
Lightning Source LLC
Chambersburg PA
CBHW060343290526
45791CB00004B/1508